BODY WARRIORS

Lisa Trumbauer

www.raintreepublishers.co.uk
Visit our website to find out more information about **Raintree** books.

To order:
☎ Phone 44 (0) 1865 888112
▤ Send a fax to 44 (0) 1865 314091
▢ Visit the Raintree bookshop at **www.raintreepublishers.co.uk** to browse our catalogue and order online.

First published in Great Britain by Raintree, Halley Court, Jordan Hill, Oxford OX2 8EJ, part of Harcourt Education.
Raintree is a registered trademark of Harcourt Education Ltd.

© Harcourt Education Ltd 2007
First published in paperback 2007
The moral right of the proprietor has been asserted.

Editorial: Louise Galpine and Harriet Milles
Design: Michelle Lisseter and Bigtop
Picture Research: Mica Brancic and Maria Joannou
Production: Camilla Crask

Originated by Modern Age
Printed and bound in China by WKT Company Limited

10-digit ISBN 1 406 20472 2 (hardback)
13-digit ISBN 978 1 4062 0472 8
11 10 09 08 07
10 9 8 7 6 5 4 3 2 1

10-digit ISBN 1 406 20497 8 (paperback)
13-digit ISBN 978 1 4062 0497 1
11 10 09 08 07
10 9 8 7 6 5 4 3 2 1

British Library
Cataloguing in Publication Data
Trumbauer, Lisa
Body warriors. - (Fusion): Immune system
614.4'7
A full catalogue record for this book is available from the British Library.

Acknowledgements
The publishers would like to thank the following for permission to reproduce photographs: Getty Images **pp. 5** (Science Faction), **12** (Taxi), **19** (Stock Image), **21** (The Image Bank), **25** (Iconica), **27** (Photonica); Corbis **pp. 10** (Thom Lang), **12** (Nieth/Zefa), **28–29** (Visuals Unlimited); Public Health Image Library **pp. 7** (Frank Collins), **8** (Janice Carr); Science Photo Library **pp. 9** top, **16** (Alfred Pasieka), **9** bottom (Volker Steger/Christian Bardele), **15** (Eye of Science), **20** (Dr Linda Stannard, UCT), **23**.

Cover photograph of T-lymphocyte killer cells (blue) attacking a cancer cell (red, ctr), reproduced with permission of Science Photo Library/Jim Dowdalls.

Every effort has been made to contact copyright holders of any material reproduced in this book. Any omissions will be rectified in subsequent printings if notice is given to the publishers.

The publishers would like to thank Nancy Harris and Harold Pratt for their assistance with the preparation of this book.

Disclaimer
All the Internet addresses (URLs) given in this book were valid at the time of going to press. However, due to the dynamic nature of the Internet, some addresses may have changed, or sites may have changed or ceased to exist since publication. While the author and publishers regret any inconvenience this may cause readers, no responsibility for any such changes can be accepted by either the author or the publishers.

It is recommended that adults supervise children on the Internet.

Contents

Some words are printed in bold, **like this**. You can find out what they mean on page 30. You can also look in the box at the bottom of the page where they first appear.

Under attack!

It might start with a tiny tickle in your throat. Soon, you start to sniffle. You begin to sneeze. Your body feels achy. Oh, no! You are getting sick. Your body is under attack!

Your body is being attacked by **germs**. Germs are tiny living creatures. Germs can cause disease. They are so tiny that you can only see them with a **microscope**. A microscope makes tiny things look much bigger.

To fight off this attack of germs, your body has two layers of **defence**. These two layers protect you from harm. They are always in action. They are your body's warriors. They fight battles inside your body every day. They also fight battles outside your body.

Sneezing is often a ▶ symptom, or sign, of being sick.

defence	protection from harm
germ	tiny living creature that can cause disease
microscope	something that helps you see very tiny things
symptom	sign that you are sick

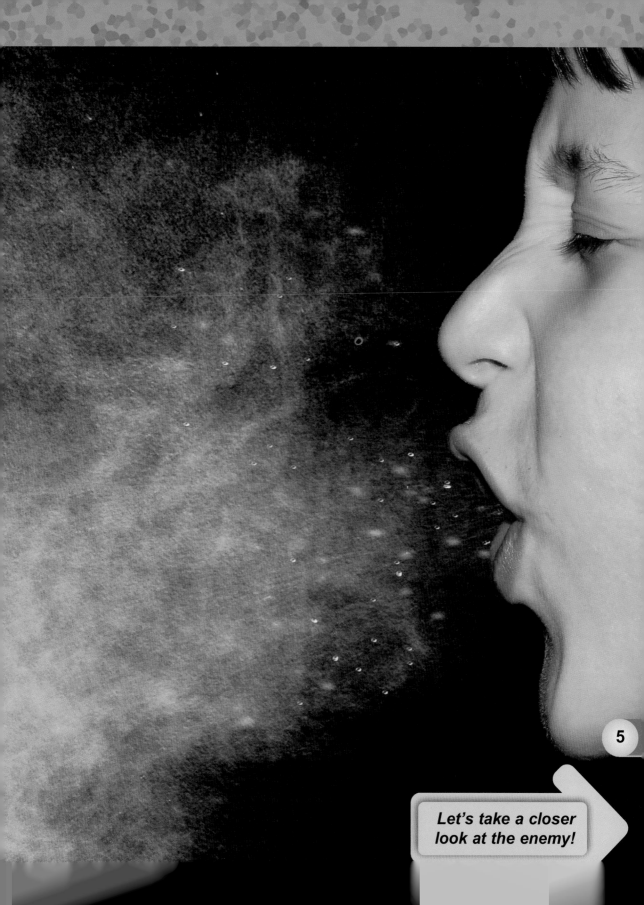

Let's take a closer look at the enemy!

Meet the enemy

Your body's enemies are **germs.** Germs can cause disease. Many germs need to live in warm, wet places. Your body is a perfect home for them.

The germs try to enter your body. They try to take over. When they take over, you get sick. Germs can cause illnesses. They can cause measles, chicken pox, and the common cold.

Germ attack!

Here are some ways that germs get into your body:

- *They can get into your body through a cut on your skin.*
- *You might breathe in germs through your mouth or nose.*
- *Germs can be in the foods you eat.*
- *Animals such as mosquitoes might carry germs. They can pass them on to you.*
- *Friends or family members might carry germs. They can pass them on to you.*

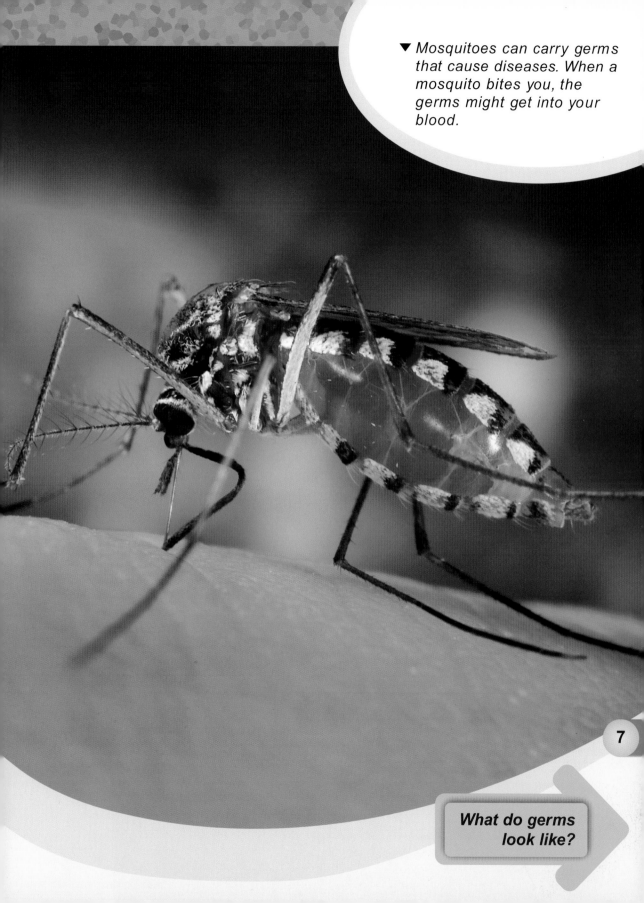

▼ Mosquitoes can carry germs that cause diseases. When a mosquito bites you, the germs might get into your blood.

What do germs look like?

Scary!

Germs are **micro-organisms**. A micro-organism is a tiny living thing. It is too small to see without a **microscope**. Even though micro-organisms are tiny, they look scary!

There are three main types of germs. These are **bacteria**, **viruses**, and **protists**.

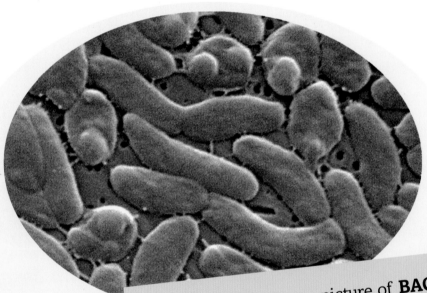

1) This is a microscope picture of **BACTERIA**. Bacteria are creatures with one **cell**. Cells are the building blocks of all living things.

bacteria	tiny living things that can cause disease
cell	building block of all living things
micro-organism	living thing that can only be seen with a microscope
protist	type of living thing with one cell
virus	tiny living thing in a cell that can cause disease

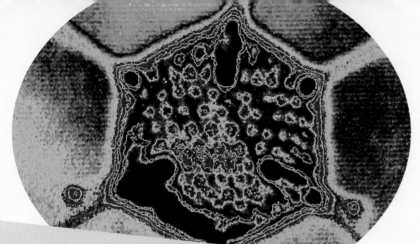

2) This is a microscope picture of a **VIRUS**. Viruses are smaller than bacteria. A virus lives inside a cell.

3) This is a microscope picture of a **PROTIST**. Protists are bigger than bacteria. You can see some protists without a microscope. Protists also have only one cell.

So, how does your body fight off these germs?

First line of defence

Your body's first line of **defence** is its outer layer. It is your skin. Your skin is an **organ**. An organ is a part of your body that does a certain job. The skin's job is to protect the inside of your body.

Your skin is pretty tough! **Germs** cannot usually break through it. But there are times when germs can get through. For example, if you have cut your skin. Then germs can enter through the broken skin.

Germ defence!

What can you do when you get a cut? The cut will slowly heal and new skin will form. While you heal, you can cover the cut with a plaster. Keep the plaster clean. A clean plaster will hold back germs.

Skin is your body's ▶ largest organ.

organ part of your body that does a certain job

Your skin does not work alone!

Germs can enter your ▼ body through your nose, mouth, and ears.

Yuck!

Germs will try many ways to get into your body. They will try to get in through your mouth. They will try to get in your nose and ears! Your body has **defences** here, too.

Your nose

Your nose has tiny hairs in it. The hairs trap germs. When you breathe out, the hairs push the germs out. The lining in your nose makes slimy stuff. It is called **mucus**. The mucus traps germs.

Your mouth

Your throat also makes a thin layer of slimy mucus. Germs can get stuck here.

Your ears

Your ears make earwax. Like mucus, earwax traps germs.

Germ defence!

*If you catch a cold, you do not want to spread it to your friends or family. So, when you cough or sneeze, cover your mouth. Use a tissue. Then throw the tissue – and the cold **viruses** – away.*

What happens if germs get past your first layer of defence?

mucus   slimy liquid inside your nose and throat

Second line of defence

A **germ** has got past your body's outer layer of **defence**. Now, your second layer of defence goes into action.

The second layer of defence is your **immune system**. It protects your body from germs. Your immune system is made up mostly of **white blood cells**. White blood cells are your inner body warriors!

White blood cells float through your blood. Their main job is to fight germs. They can recognize a harmful germ. Then they go into action!

Red blood cells also float through your blood. Red blood cells carry **oxygen**. Oxygen is a gas in the air. Your body needs oxygen to survive.

Red blood cells look like ▶ doughnuts or tyres. The white blood cell in this picture looks spiky. White blood cells can take on different shapes.

immune system	system in your body that protects you from germs
oxygen	gas in the air that most living things need
red blood cell	part of the blood that carries oxygen (the gas you breathe)
white blood cell	part of the blood that protects your body from harmful germs

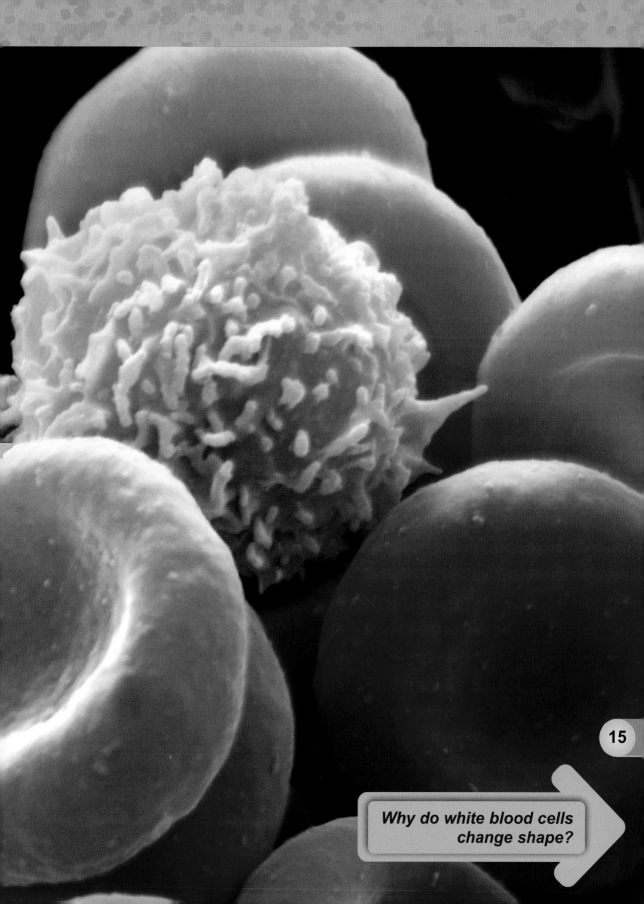

Why do white blood cells change shape?

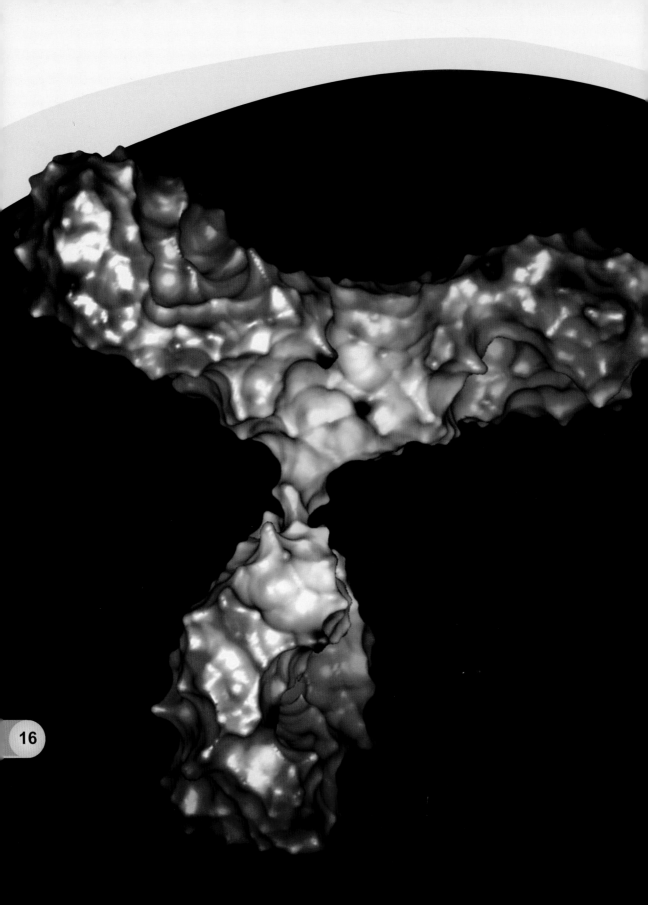

Time to go to work

Your body has five types of **white blood cells**. So, how do these **cells** protect you from harmful **germs**?

Most white blood cells gather near the walls of **blood vessels**. A blood vessel is a narrow tube in your body. Blood flows through it. A germ may have got into your blood.

White blood cells can move through the walls of some blood vessels. They can change their shape to get through. If a germ gets in, the white blood cells swallow it up. They destroy it!

Some white blood cells release **antibodies**. Antibodies are substances that fight diseases. Germs do not like antibodies. They will move away from antibodies. They will group together. Then, the white blood cells can get to the germs more easily. They can destroy them.

◀ *This antibody is shaped like the letter* Y.

antibody   substance in your body that fights off disease
blood vessel narrow tube in your body that blood flows through

Let us in!

It's a busy day. You are not thinking about **germs**. But they are out there! They are looking for a way into your body.

Germs can enter your body through a cut on your skin. They try to get in through your nose or mouth. They hope that your first line of **defence** will be weak.

Your skin fights back. The slimy **mucus** and tiny hairs in your nose fight back.

But some germs can still get in. They are the **viruses** that cause the common cold. Ugh! The cold viruses have got through your body's first layer of defence.

Maybe you cut your skin on a rock? ▶ Maybe your friend is sneezing? Cold viruses could be moving through the air. Watch out! Germs are looking for a way in.

How does the
virus get in?

Sick!

You feel rough! Your throat hurts. You are sneezing. You start to cough. Your whole body aches. You know these **symptoms**, or signs. You know you have a cold.

Cold **viruses** travel through the air. They often travel in tiny drops of water. Most likely the cold viruses entered your body through your nose. Then, they stuck to the slimy **mucus** in your nose and throat. But some of the viruses got through your **defences**. They entered your blood.

*This is a **microscope*** ▶
photo of the viruses
that cause colds.

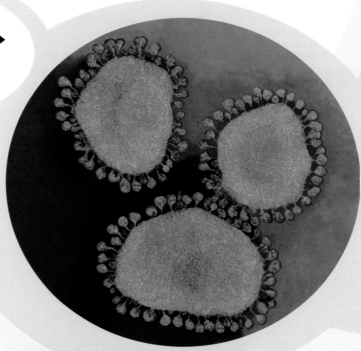

fever	body temperature that is higher than normal
temperature	measure of how hot or cold something is
thermometer	instrument that measures heat or cold

▲ Sometimes a cold gives you a **fever**. Fevers happen when your body **temperature** goes above 37 ºC (98.6 ºF). A **thermometer** measures your body's temperature.

How does your body fight back?

The battle

The cold **viruses** have entered your blood. Now your **white blood cells** go into action. White blood cells are a part of the blood. They protect you from harmful **germs**.

Your white blood cells fight the viruses. They battle until all the germs are gone. This battle often takes several days. That is why a cold may last for a while.

While you are sick, your white blood cells swallow up the cold viruses. These warriors defend your body. During this fight, your body needs to rest. The white blood cells help you to feel better again.

Toxins

*Some germs give off **toxins**. Toxins are poisons. They can make you sick. Some white blood cells give off **antitoxins**. Antitoxins stop harmful toxins.*

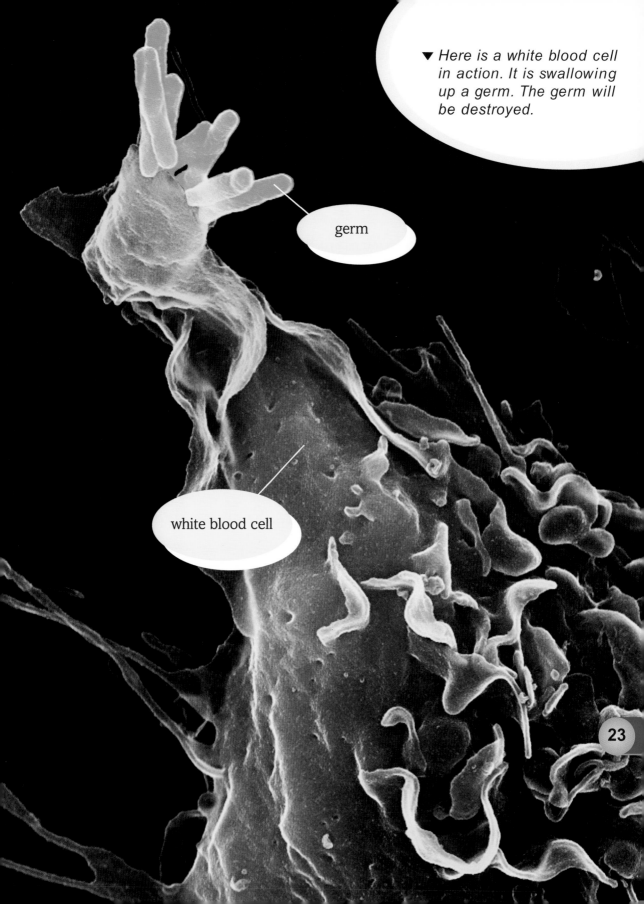

Here is a white blood cell in action. It is swallowing up a germ. The germ will be destroyed.

germ

white blood cell

Victory!

Ah! Slowly, you start to feel better. Your throat does not hurt so much. Your nose stops running. Your body does not ache any more. Your **fever** is gone.

Your **white blood cells** have done their job. They have protected your body from **germs**. They have killed the cold **viruses** that invaded your body.

Cold medicine

Over 200 different viruses cause the common cold. Some people take medicine to help fight a cold. Medicine can help, but not much. Scientists have not yet invented a medicine that can stop every single cold virus. Your body's white blood cells are better at fighting the cold virus than any medicine.

Your white blood cells▶ have won the battle. It is great to feel better!

Another line of defence: you

You can help your body's **defences**. **Germs** can stay on your skin. Washing your body helps get rid of germs. Eating well keeps your body healthy. Exercising keeps your body healthy, too.

A healthy body means your **immune system** is always ready. It is ready to attack any germs.

Your body can handle most harmful germs. The outer layer of defence keeps many germs from getting in. If germs do get through, your immune system attacks. It destroys the harmful germs.

Your body's warriors are always standing guard. They are always working hard to protect you.

Keeping your skin ▶ clean can stop germs from getting through.

Your incredible blood

Your blood is amazing. **Red blood cells** carry **oxygen** around your body. Oxygen is the gas your body needs to survive. **White blood cells** are your **immune system**. They protect your body from **germs**. They know when a harmful germ has entered your body. They fight to destroy it.

One drop of blood can have between 7,000 and 25,000 white blood cells. There are about one billion red blood cells in just a few drops of blood.

Red blood cells carry oxygen (the gas you breathe).

White blood cells protect your body from harmful germs. They are usually bigger than red blood cells. There are fewer white blood cells than red blood cells.

Some white blood cells can actually remember a harmful germ. If a harmful germ appears again, the white blood cells can remember how to destroy it. That is why people only get some illnesses once, such as chicken pox.

White blood cells are not really white. They have no colour at all.

Glossary

antibody substance in your body that fights off disease

antitoxin substance in your body that fights off toxins (poisons)

bacteria tiny living things that can cause disease

blood vessel narrow tube in your body that blood flows through

cell building block of all living things

defence protection from harm

fever body temperature that is higher than normal

germ tiny living creature that can cause disease

immune system system in your body that protects you from germs. White blood cells are an important part of the body's immune system.

micro-organism living thing that can only be seen with a microscope. Germs are a type of micro-organism.

microscope something that helps you see very tiny things. Scientists use microscopes to look at germs.

mucus slimy liquid inside your nose and throat

organ part of your body that does a certain job. Skin is the largest organ in the human body.

oxygen gas in the air that most living things need. Oxygen has no taste, colour, or smell.

protist type of living thing with one cell

red blood cell part of the blood that carries oxygen (the gas you breathe). Most blood cells are red blood cells.

symptom sign that you are sick

temperature measure of how hot or cold something is

thermometer instrument that measures heat or cold

toxin poison

virus tiny living thing in a cell that can cause disease

white blood cell part of the blood that protects your body from harmful germs

Want to know more?

Books to read

- *Body Focus: The Immune System*, Carol Ballard (Heinemann Library, 2003)
- *Microlife: From Amoebas to Viruses*, Claybourne, Anna (Heinemann Library, 2004)
- *Body Talk: Defend Yourself*, Steve Parker (Raintree, 2006)

Websites

- http://yahooligans.yahoo.com/content/ask_earl
  Ask Earl on the Yahooligans website to learn more about diseases and how they make you sick.
- http://kidshealth.org/kid
  Find out how to look after your body, eat healthily, and stay fit!

Read more about the micro-organisms that cause disease in *World's Worst Germs*.

To see what your body parts can do when they are working well, read *Are You Tough Enough?*

Index